""CEO Chronicles: Inside the Executive Diary"

Fred T. Bryant

Introduction:

Beginning the journey

A fascinating view into the life of a Chief Executive Officer (CEO), "CEO Chronicles" is. In these pages, you'll learn what it's truly like to run a business and the personal journey that goes along with such a significant position.

The CEO's Changing Role

CEOs are more than just revenue and profit. In the competitive corporate environment of today, they are organizations' leaders, visionaries, and motivators. They must solve complicated problems, encourage innovation, and negotiate the complexity of a global marketplace.

The Humanity of the CEO

CEOs' polished personas conceal a personal narrative. Like everyone else, they have doubts, vulnerable times, and personal sacrifices. The show "CEO Chronicles" shows us this human side of leadership and serves as a reminder that even the most successful individuals experience difficulties.

The Influence of Introspection

This journal offers a distinctive perspective on the process of self-reflection. CEOs can learn a lot by analyzing their thoughts and behaviors. The publication "CEO Chronicles" extends this technique by providing uncensored access to a CEO's daily musings and opinions.

Getting Around the Journey

Each chapter of the book corresponds to a stage in a CEO's career. You will begin with their early years and formative experiences before delving into the high-stakes decision-making environment. Explore their position as visionaries and the personal costs they bear in order to succeed professionally after that.

The Revelation

As you read "CEO Chronicles," you'll see successes and weaknesses, intelligent choices and unsure times. This journal demonstrates how a CEO's ideals, impact, and extraordinary journey are just as important to define as their title.

Let's start

Prepare for this incredible voyage as "CEO Chronicles" explores the fundamentals of leadership in the twenty-first century. Welcome to a fresh look at the CEO's world.

Chapter 1

.Creating a Vision

The CEO Chronicles: Personal Essays
One of the most challenging yet rewarding duties in the realm of business leadership is heading up a platoon. The "CEO Chronicles" book's chapter "Leading the Team" delves into the specifics of this crucial role, outlining the strategies, challenges, and insight that CEOs employ to lead their organizations to success.

The practice of guiding, inspiring, and influencing people or a group to work together toward a single goal or vision is an essential component of leadership. Leadership is a difficult concept that is crucial in a variety of areas of life, including business, politics, education, and community organizations. The following crucial elements emphasize how important leadership is.

1. Establishing a course By establishing aspirations, goals, and a vision, leaders provide their platoon or company with a clear sense of direction. They describe the requirements and the significance of each.

2. Provocation and allusion by powerful leaders can inspire and motivate their subordinates. They provide the squad members a witching vision that arouses their zeal and loyalty and inspires them to go above and beyond.

3.Leaders are expected to make sensible decisions consistently in challenging situations with unknown outcomes. Their suggestions can influence the course of action and foster a culture of responsibility within their unit.

4. Responsibility Leaders are accountable for the outcomes of their decisions and actions. They encourage a culture of

accountability within their unit and take ownership of both successes and shortcomings.

5. Suitable Interaction The foundation of good leadership is communication. Leaders must successfully communicate their research, aspirations, and review to a wide range of people. Effective communication fosters understanding and trust.

6.Conflict Resolution Managing disagreements and conflicts within a team or organization is a responsibility of leadership. By handling problems in a constructive manner, effective leaders may maintain a positive work environment.

7. Establishing and fostering relationships Connections based on mutual respect and trust are fostered by effective leaders. By promoting a sense of unity and cohesion, they promote platoon members' camaraderie and collaboration.

8. Stability Leaders need to adapt in order to deal with changing issues and situations. They exhibit rigor and adaptability while leading their battalion through changes and heads.

9. Other People's Development Effective leaders go out of their way to aid their unit members in moving forward. They provide literacy opportunities, support people in realizing their full potential, and assist them in understanding their flaws and strengths.

10. Creativity and problem-solving Leaders encourage creativity and innovation by fostering an environment where platoon members feel comfortable bringing up novel generalizations and findings. They are flexible and keen to try out novel approaches to solving issues.

11. Integrity of Action Leadership should be guided by strict ethical standards. Leaders

set an example by conducting themselves honestly, fairly, and morally.

12. Visionary Permission Effective leaders are able to see beyond the immediate issues at hand. They inspire others to work toward that common goal because they envisage a better future.

13. Crisis management Leaders provide stability and guidance during difficult times. They make difficult decisions while upholding the group's will to face difficulties.

In conclusion, the crucial role of leadership is to steer groups of people and organizations in the right direction by creating a vision, fostering cooperation, and successfully overcoming obstacles. There are many different types of capacities in leadership.

Chapter 2

Leading the Teams:

The CEO Chronicles: Personal Essays

One of the most challenging yet rewarding duties in the realm of business leadership is leading a team. The "Leading the Team" chapter in the "CEO Chronicles" book delves into the specifics of this vital role, revealing the strategies, challenges, and insights that CEOs employ to lead their businesses to success.

The process of guiding, inspiring, and influencing people or a group to work together toward a single goal or vision is the primary function of leadership. Leadership is a difficult concept that is essential in a variety of areas of life, including business, politics, education, and community organizations. The importance of leadership is shown by the following major factors:

1.Setting Direction: By establishing goals, objectives, and a vision, leaders provide their team or organization a clear sense of direction. They describe what has to be done and why it is crucial.

2.Inspiration and Motivation: Strong leaders inspire and encourage their teams. They enthuse team members with a compelling vision, fuel their zeal and commitment, and encourage them to go above and beyond.

3.Decision-Making: Leaders are required to make sensible decisions, often in difficult and unforeseeable situations. Their choices can shape the future and encourage a culture of accountability within their team.

4. Accountability: Leaders are accountable for the outcomes of their decisions and actions. They encourage a culture of accountability within their team and take ownership of both successes and failures.

5. Effective Communication: Effective communication is the foundation of leadership. In order to effectively convey people's opinions, objectives, and critiques, leaders must pay close attention to what they are saying. Effective communication fosters understanding and trust.

6. Conflict Resolution: Leadership requires managing disputes and conflicts within a team or organization. By handling conflicts in a positive way, effective leaders can maintain a positive work environment.

7.Building and Nurturing Relationships: Strong leaders encourage ties built on trust and respect. They establish a sense of unity and cohesion among the team members, which promotes cooperation and camaraderie.

8. Adaptability: Leaders must change to address new issues and situations. They demonstrate flexibility and resilience as they guide their team through changes and emergencies.

9.Development of Others: Effective leaders work to promote team members. They provide learning opportunities, assist people in realizing their full potential, and assist them in understanding their strengths and weaknesses.

10.Innovation and Problem-Solving: Leaders encourage creativity and innovation by fostering an environment where team members feel at ease bringing forth original ideas and solutions. They are flexible and keen to try out novel approaches to problem-solving.

11.Ethical Conduct: Leadership should be guided by high ethical standards. By acting and making decisions with integrity, honesty, and fairness, leaders establish an example for others to follow.

12. Visionary Thinking: Successful leaders are able to see beyond the immediate issues at hand. They inspire others to work toward the same objective because they envisage a better future.

13. Crisis management: Leaders provide guidance and stability during difficult times. They make challenging decisions and uphold the group's dedication to overcoming obstacles.

In conclusion, the crucial role of leadership is to steer groups of people and organizations in the right direction by creating a vision, fostering cooperation, and successfully overcoming challenges. Leadership consists of a variety of skills and qualities that may be developed and adapted to different contexts; it is not limited to a certain style or approach.

Making and Managing High-Performing Teams Is the Key to Success

Collaboration is frequently the secret to success in the corporate world. The strategies, challenges, and importance of creating teams that perform above and beyond expectations are thoroughly examined in this inquiry.

Why Successful Teams Are Vital

Individuals who get along well together develop teams that work well. Their combined strengths make each other even better, creating a whole that is greater than the sum of its parts. These teams are crucial to the success of a company because they are not just efficient but also imaginative, creative, and motivated.

Team Dynamics: How Teams Work

If you want to build a high-performing team, it is crucial to understand how teams function. Teams go through many stages as they grow, from getting to know one another to operating well. Teams may have challenges like conflicts and confusion about duties, but effective management can help them get through these phases.

Selecting the Best Team Members

The first step in creating a high-performing team is selecting the right people. Cultural fit should be considered together with talents during the hiring process. The team's members should get along well and share the company's values.

Diversity and Inclusion

The most creative solutions are usually created by diverse teams with people from a variety of backgrounds and areas of expertise. When leading diverse teams, inclusive leadership is necessary for everyone to feel heard and valued.

Clarifying Roles and Objectives

Defined responsibilities and clear objectives are essential for a high-performing team. Each team member needs to be aware of what is expected of them and how their contribution fits into the overall scheme.

Building a Culture of Collaboration

Collaboration is essential for productive teamwork. Building a collaborative culture requires promoting open communication, idea exchange, and cross-functional work.

What a Leader Does

A key component of high-performing teams is the leadership. Effective leaders know how to encourage and inspire their teams. Key characteristics of effective leaders are emotional intelligence, empathy, and active listening.

Feedback and Resolution of Conflict
Working in a team inevitably involves conflict. Open communication about disagreements is essential, as is offering helpful criticism to spur development.

Developing and empowering team members
Teams with high performance are constantly changing. Leaders serve as coaches and mentors, assisting team members in developing their skills and taking advantage of educational opportunities.

Recognizing Successes
Any victory should be celebrated since it improves team spirit and strengthens the culture of excellence.

Keeping the Team Together
For good performance, a team needs to be cohesive. Leadership through trying times and team-building exercises aid in

preserving a sense of cohesion and purpose.

Resilience and Flexibility
Teams that operate well are flexible and resilient to change. They see difficulties as chances for development and innovation.

The Effects of High-Performing Teams
Teams that function well are not only productive but also transformative. They produce amazing outcomes, promote creativity, and fuel success. Such teams require constant development and management, which is a journey filled with opportunity. High-performing teams act as pillars of achievement in a collaborative environment.

Wisdom from the Front Lines of Influence: Leadership Lessons
Both an art and a science, leadership is developed by experiences, obstacles, and a never-ending desire for progress. In this

in-depth investigation, we delve into the complex world of leadership and unearth insightful insights from illustrious individuals, seasoned leaders, and pivotal occasions in the history of impact.

Introduction: The Dynamic World of Leadership

Leadership is a dynamic field that must continually adjust to circumstances and times that are changing. Effective leadership goes beyond the conventional top-down approach in today's fast-paced and interconnected environment. It involves motivating followers, being flexible, and encouraging a feeling of purpose in them.

Lesson 1: The Power of Authenticity and Leading by Example

Authenticity is the key to effective leadership. The trust and respect of their teams are won by leaders who set the example by upholding their beliefs and acting with uncompromising honesty. This course examines the value of authenticity in leadership and the ways in which it motivates others to emulate it.

Lesson 2: Charting a Clear Path under Visionary Leadership
Visionary leaders are able to inspire their followers' passion and dedication by clearly communicating their vision of the future. This session digs into the practice of visionary leadership, highlighting the value of establishing a clear course of action and motivating others to follow suit.

Lesson 3: The Heart of Effective Leadership: Emotional Intelligence
Successful leaders have emotional intelligence (EQ), which is a defining quality. The crucial function of EQ in leadership is examined in this course, from self-awareness and self-control through empathy and social skills. Leaders that have a high EQ are able to negotiate

interpersonal situations deftly and create happier workplaces.

Lesson 4: Leading Through Change and Adaptability
Adaptability is a leadership superpower in today's world of rapid change. This session goes in-depth on the value of accepting change and guiding teams through changes. It looks at methods for keeping things calm during tumultuous times and making sure that change is handled with resiliency rather than opposition.

lesson 5: Communication The Art of Influence,
The foundation of leadership is good communication. This course examines a number of communication-related topics, including non-verbal clues, persuasive speaking, and active listening. It highlights the need of empathic, succinct communication in fostering trust and agreement.

Lesson 6: Servant Leadership – Prioritizing Others

By focusing on the leader's responsibility to meet the needs of others, servant leadership flips the conventional leadership paradigm on its head. This course explores the idea of servant leadership and demonstrates how leaders who put their team's welfare first develop devoted and driven followers.

Lesson 7: Creating and Managing Effective Teams

Beyond an individual's skills, leadership includes the capacity to create and manage high-performing teams. This session examines the methods for putting together diverse teams, outlining specific objectives, and encouraging a collaborative environment.

Lesson 8: Steadfast in the Storm: Leading Through Crisis

The ultimate leadership challenges are presented in times of crisis. This course explores the qualities of leaders who maintain composure, decisiveness, and empathy under pressure. It emphasizes that good crisis leadership is about negotiating misfortune with grace rather than trying to escape it.

Lesson 9: The Moral Compass in Ethical Leadership

Leadership that is morally upright is essential, not optional. This course explores the ethical dilemmas that leaders frequently encounter as well as the values that underpin moral judgment. It underlines how ethical executives set a norm for behavior throughout their entire organization.

Lesson 10: Being Resilient and Overcoming Adversity

Leaders have failures and losses, but what distinguishes them is their resiliency. The significance of resilience in leadership and techniques for enhancing mental toughness are discussed in this lesson. Leaders that are resilient seize opportunities from challenges and motivate others to do the same.

Lesson 11: The Road to Mastery Through Continuous Learning

The journey of leadership is not its end point. The need of lifelong learning for leaders is emphasized in this lesson. It covers a range of topics for lifelong learning, including mentorship, self-reflection, seeking criticism, and remaining open to new ideas.

Lesson 12: Motivating People and Leaving a Legacy

True leaders can be identified by the legacy they leave behind. The last lesson considers how leadership affects people, groups, and society as a whole. It demonstrates that being a leader is about inspiring others to stand up and carry the flame forward as well as about achieving personal achievement.

The Never-Ending Search for Leadership Excellence

As we come to a close with our investigation of "Leadership Lessons," we acknowledge that leadership is a dynamic and developing discipline. It involves utilizing the strength of vision, emotional intelligence, adaptability, and honesty. It has to do with ethics, teamwork, communication, and service. It is about perseverance, ongoing education, and motivating others to achieve success.

Leadership is a skill that can be developed by people at all levels of a company; it is not just the realm of CEOs and executives. Influence and impact are more important than titles and power.

It's crucial to learn and put these principles into practice since leadership affects how companies and society develop. Leadership is a journey, one that involves development, giving back, and making a difference. Every lesson we learn advances us closer to becoming the leaders the world needs. The pursuit of leadership greatness is never-ending.

Chapter 3

Facing Challenges:

A Complete Guide to Surviving Difficult Situations and Succeeding

Challenges are the threads that connect our experiences of development, resiliency, and victory in the tapestry of life. They are the challenges, disappointments, and difficulties that put our resolve to the test and mold our futures. This in-depth investigation aims to define and clarify the science and art of overcoming obstacles, providing a thorough manual for using adversity as a springboard for both individual and collective development.

Defining Obstacles as a Natural Aspect of Life

In essence, challenges are circumstances or impediments that present problems and necessitate answers. They might appear in a variety of ways, including external issues like money problems or professional losses as well as interior concerns like self-doubt or emotional distress. No one is exempt from the ups and downs of life's difficulties, regardless of the variety in the form and size of problems.

Challenges' Dynamic Nature

Challenges are not static; they change as we go through life, evolving, morphing, and adapting. It is essential to comprehend their dynamic character in order to navigate them successfully. Challenges are not insurmountable hurdles, but rather chances for development, resiliency, and self-discovery, whether they take the form of interpersonal conflicts, professional difficulties, or societal disasters.

Challenges' Psychological Environment

At their foundation, challenges are psychological experiences that elicit a range of feelings and reactions rather than merely being physical events. Challenges frequently come with anxiety, tension, fear, and sometimes despair, which affects our mental and emotional health. The first step in successfully managing obstacles is to identify and deal with their psychological components.

resilience and is frequently regarded as the key to overcoming obstacles
It is a trait that enables people to endure setbacks, adjust to change, and overcome difficulties stronger than before. Understanding and embracing resilience is a crucial step in preparing oneself to face life's challenges.

How to Develop a Growth Mindset
A growth mindset is the idea that aptitudes and intelligence can be increased through commitment and effort, according to psychologist Carol Dweck. A crucial strategy for dealing with difficulties is to adopt a growth mindset, which encourages people to see failures as opportunities for

improvement. The development of this mindset prepares people to navigate obstacles in a proactive and resilient manner.

The Art and Science of Overcoming Obstacles in Problem-Solving

The practical side of addressing problems is problem-solving. It entails determining the issue, deconstructing it, coming up with potential solutions, and acting decisively. A ability that enables people to approach problems methodically and with confidence is effective problem-solving.

Making Decisions in an Uncertain World

Making crucial judgments, sometimes in the midst of uncertainty, is a common requirement of challenges. Making decisions involves clarity, reason, and the capacity to balance risks and rewards, especially in trying circumstances. It is an essential tool for overcoming obstacles and can have an impact on both personal and professional achievements.

Managing Stress: Weathering the Storm Calmly

Challenges inevitably bring stress, and preserving physical and mental wellbeing requires excellent stress management. Techniques like mindfulness, meditation, exercise, and time management are effective techniques for reducing the negative impacts of stress and improving one's ability to handle obstacles gracefully.

The Function of Safety Nets

Challenging situations are rarely navigated alone. Friends, family, mentors, and communities all serve as important support networks that offer emotional, social, and even practical assistance. Developing and utilizing these support networks is like having a lifeline when things go tough.

Getting Rid of Fear and Putting Things Off

On the road to overcoming obstacles, fear and procrastination are deadly foes. It is crucial to comprehend the psychology underlying these challenges and put methods in place to overcome them. The secret to growth is taking bold action in the face of fear and acting quickly when procrastination is there.

Searching for and absorbing knowledge from others

People who have overcome obstacles and succeeded throughout history have left behind invaluable lessons. For people facing comparable difficulties, studying the insights and experiences of these role models and taking inspiration from their experiences can be a source of inspiration and direction.

The Power of Challenges to Transform
Challenges are more than just obstacles to go through; they are catalysts for change. They may result in significant personal development, self-awareness, and a greater comprehension of one's potential and purpose. To overcome obstacles with resiliency and knowledge, it is essential to recognize and utilize this transforming potential.

Conclusion: The Path Through Difficulties
As we come to a close with our in-depth investigation of "Navigating Through Challenges," we realize that obstacles are not enemies to be vanquished but rather essential components of the human experience. They provide the blank canvas for us to paint the tapestry of our lives, molding us into stronger, more compassionate, and more self-aware people.

It takes a team to successfully navigate obstacles, and along the process, vital lessons are acquired. It serves as the furnace where character is developed, potential is realized, and the human spirit triumphs. Challenges are milestones in our life's adventure, not their final destination.

Chapter 4

.A CEO's Daily Life

A CEO's Daily Life: Juggling Vision, Leadership, and Decision-Making
The Chief Executive Officer (CEO) position is tough and diverse, including a complicated jumble of duties, difficulties, and decision-making. This in-depth investigation will reveal the complex web of a CEO's daily activities, providing a thorough understanding of their routine, decision-making procedures, and the particular difficulties they face.

Introduction: The Crucible of the CEO
Although the life of a CEO is frequently admired, it is actually a world of constant responsibility and decision-making. The position entails much more than just board meetings and corner offices. It involves

leadership, planning, and steadfast dedication to the mission of the organization.

Chapter 1: The Morning Routine,
The CEO typically starts their day early. We'll discuss the standard morning routine, which may include physical activity, meditation, or a nutritious breakfast to get the day started. Many CEOs appreciate this calm period for contemplation and planning.

Chapter 2: The Information Flux
CEOs receive a constant barrage of information from different sources, including emails, reports, news updates, and more. Daily management of this influx is difficult. We'll dig into methods for swiftly processing information.

Chapter 3: Engaging Leadership Teams in
In order to determine priorities and synchronize strategy, CEOs collaborate closely with their leadership teams. To keep

everyone on the same page, department leaders and executives must meet frequently.

Chapter 4: The CEO's Primary Duty: Decision-Making
Making important decisions takes up a large portion of a CEO's day. We'll look at how decisions are made, including acquiring information, analyzing our options, and taking the long view.

Chapter 5: Visionary Leadership,
The company's vision must be developed and communicated by the CEO. We'll talk about how they energize and encourage staff to collaborate on common objectives.

Chapter 6 : Management of Crises,
The life of a CEO is filled with obstacles and catastrophes. This chapter explores how CEOs deal with unforeseen circumstances, make difficult choices under duress, and reassure stakeholders.

Chapter 7: External Engagements,
CEOs frequently interact with outside parties, including as clients, partners, and investors. We'll look at how they create and keep up these vital connections.

Chapter 8: Effective Time Management
For CEOs, time management is essential. It takes a certain amount of skill to juggle several obligations while staying focused on strategic concerns.

Chapter 9: Lifelong Learning and Personal Development
CEOs are aware of the value of personal development. We'll talk about how they schedule time for self-improvement and keep up with business developments.

Chapter 10: Work-Life Balance (or Lack Thereof)
The pressures of being a CEO might make it difficult to distinguish between business

and personal life. We'll talk about their attempts to keep some sort of equilibrium.

Chapter 11: The Function of Delegation
CEOs cannot accomplish everything by themselves. We'll look at how CEOs assign responsibilities to their staff because delegation is a crucial skill.

Chapter 12: the evening routine and reflection
The workday does not always mark the conclusion of a CEO's day. We'll have a look at their nightly habits, which could include assessing the day's successes and making plans for the following day.

The CEO's Odyssey's conclusion
The life of a CEO is characterized by leadership, vision, and the constant ebb and flow of challenges and decisions. It is a tireless pursuit of organizational greatness. There is a great deal of dedication and passion to a company's success hidden

behind the boardroom discussions and public appearances. CEOs have a heavy burden of duty because they are passionate about the goals of their companies.

Although their jobs may be stressful, CEOs feel satisfaction in leading their organizations to success. It is a role that calls for unflinching commitment and tenacity and is evidence of the unbreakable spirit of leadership. CEOs continue to be the guiding lights in the ever-changing corporate world, steering their firms through the challenges of the contemporary era.

Chapter 5

Staying Innovative

The CEO Chronicles' guiding principle is to be innovative.

The "CEO Chronicles" is more than simply a book; it takes the reader on an engrossing journey into the world of inspiring visionaries, clever decision-making, and the unrelenting quest of excellence. The ageless notion of innovation is at the heart of it. In this thorough investigation, we delve into the essence of being inventive as it is presented in the "CEO Chronicles," defining the idea and identifying the crucial tactics CEOs utilize to manage change, advance their organizations, and infuse innovation into their leadership.

Chapter 1: The Beginning of Innovation,

In the CEO Chronicles, innovation is more than just a trendy word—it's the lifeblood of development. Setting the stage, this chapter defines innovation as a persistent dedication to original concepts, flexibility, and the unrelenting quest of improvement. It emphasizes the role of innovation as the motivating factor for forward-thinking CEOs.

Chapter 2:A Dynamic Landscape of Change,

A dynamic business environment is shown in great detail in The CEO Chronicles. This chapter explores how remaining inventive in this constantly changing world is not simply a choice but a tactical need. It looks at the need for CEOs to remain aware of shifting market dynamics, technology developments, and changing client expectations.

Chapter 3: The CEO's Responsibility to Maintain Innovation

In the universe of the CEO Chronicles, innovation is a philosophy that CEOs must adopt rather than the task of a department. This chapter breaks down the elements of remaining innovative as seen from the perspective of CEOs. It highlights the importance of an innovator's attitude, adaptability, inventiveness, and curiosity as key characteristics for visionary leadership.

Chapter 4: The Curiosity, Quotient
Innovation is sparked by a curious mind. Curiosity propels CEOs to explore unexplored territory in the CEO Chronicles. This chapter explores the role of curiosity in the innovation process and provides information on how CEOs can foster and use it to encourage innovation.

Section 5: The Innovative CEO
Innovation relies heavily on creativity. CEOs in the Chronicles serve as prime examples of the creative spirit by questioning norms and fusing dissimilar concepts. This chapter examines how CEOs encourage creativity in both themselves and their businesses, providing examples of how they promote an

environment that encourages creative thinking.

Chapter 6: Leading Through Change in
In the CEO Chronicles, innovation serves as the CEO's compass for navigating change, which is a continuous companion. This chapter explores the art of adaptation and the ways in which CEOs guide their companies through change while showcasing their adaptability and fortitude in the face of ambiguity.

Chapter 7: of The CEO Chronicles: The Innovator's Mindset
The CEOs in the Chronicles represent the innovator's mindset, which combines optimism, toughness, and adaptability. This chapter explores how CEOs develop this mindset and demonstrates how it plays a part in overcoming obstacles, grabbing opportunities, and continuously promoting innovation.

Chapter 8: Innovation Maintenance Techniques

In the CEO Chronicles, innovation is a planned process; it is not the result of chance. This chapter provides useful information about the tactics CEOs use to maintain their innovativeness. It includes a variety of strategies, such as promoting an innovative culture, supporting experimentation, and respecting other points of view.

Chapter 9: Removing Barriers to Innovation

Even in the Chronicles, there are often obstacles in the way of innovation. CEOs approach and overcome these challenges with unshakable resolve. This chapter lists key innovation roadblocks, like as risk aversion and organizational bureaucracy, and offers advice on how forward-thinking CEOs might get beyond them.

Chapter 10: Collaboration: The CEO's Secret, Weapon

Collaboration is often the key to innovation's success. The CEO Chronicles provide examples of how CEOs use teamwork to fuel innovation. In order to highlight its contribution to the creative process, this chapter discusses the role of cooperation in forming interdisciplinary teams and absorbing various viewpoints.

Chapter 11: The Ethical Imperative,

Both opportunities and moral quandaries are brought on by innovation. CEOs in the Chronicles deal with these difficulties in a moral and accountable manner. This chapter explores the moral issues that accompany innovation, placing special emphasis on the CEO's responsibility for upholding moral standards in all areas—from data privacy to sustainability.

Chapter 12: of The CEO Chronicles: Measuring and Evaluating Innovation

To evaluate the effectiveness of their innovation activities, CEOs require measurements. The CEO Chronicles show CEOs evaluating innovation using a range of measurements and instruments. This chapter introduces these metrics and analyzes their applicability in assessing the performance of innovations, including ROI, market share, and customer happiness.

Chapter 13: The CEO Chronicles, The Future of Remaining Innovative
The Chronicles offer a glimpse into the technological future. This chapter examines contemporary developments, such as the fusion of technology, sustainability, and international cooperation. It emphasizes how important keeping inventive is going forward as CEOs continue to influence society.

Conclusion: The CEO Chronicles: The Endless Saga of Innovation

One truth stands out as we draw to a close this in-depth examination of remaining inventive in the CEO Chronicles: innovation is not a destination but an ongoing journey. It's an adventure propelled by curiosity, inventiveness, adaptability, and an unchanging dedication to advancement.

The Chronicles serve as a timely reminder that maintaining originality is a duty, not a choice. Instead of just keeping up, it's important to set the pace, push organizations forward, and sculpt the future. It's evidence of the innovative leadership spirit of CEOs who dare to dream, create, and lead. Innovation is the special tool of entrepreneurship, according to Peter Drucker. the process by which resources acquire a new capacity to produce value. Innovation is not merely a theme in the CEO Chronicles; it is also the essence of visionary leadership, the power behind growth, and the unwavering dedication to a more promising, innovative future.

Chapter 6

Building Relationships

Building Connections: The Science and Art of Interaction

The intricate tapestry of our life is woven from the strands of our relationships. Our relationships with our loved ones, friends, coworkers, and other acquaintances affect our experiences, our enjoyment, and our success. Relationship building is a science that can be understood and accomplished, as well as an art that incorporates the heart. In this in-depth analysis, we will define the broad idea of relationship building and break it down into its core ideas, guiding principles, and practical tactics to assist you in creating deep connections in both your personal and professional lives.

Chapter 1: The Importance of Relationships

Relationships are the core of our existence; they go beyond simple encounters. This chapter highlights the significant effects of relationships on our health, emphasizing how they bring comfort, joy, and a sense of community. It emphasizes how important connections are in shaping our futures as opposed to just being a part of life.

Chapter 2: Defining Relationship-Building

Building relationships is fundamentally about fostering and cultivating ties with other people. This chapter provides a thorough definition, highlighting that it includes building trust, encouraging respect for one another, and using good communication. It highlights the reciprocal aspect of relationships, in which both sides support and contribute to their development.

Chapter 3: The Relationship Building Foundations

Solid foundations are the building blocks of strong partnerships. The fundamental tenets of relationship development, such as respect, open communication, and trust, are explored in this chapter. It explores how these components form the foundation for stronger ties and act as the cornerstone of any meaningful connection.

Section 4: The Function of Empathy

The emotional link that forges deep connections between people is empathy. Empathy is described in this chapter as the capacity to comprehend and experience another person's feelings. It looks at how empathy fosters compassion, understanding, and genuine connections in relationships.

Chapter 5: Authenticity in Relationship Building

Building sincere and enduring connections requires authenticity. Authenticity is described in this chapter as being consistent with one's true self in one's actions, words, and values. It emphasizes that sincerity, openness, and a sincere desire to connect are the foundations of meaningful relationships.

Chapter 6: The Art of Effective Communication,

The foundation of any relationship is effective communication. This chapter explores the art of communication, including non-verbal indicators, active listening, and clear expression. It highlights how important communication is for forging bonds with others and settling disputes.

Chapter 7: BuildingProfessional Relationships,

Building relationships is essential to success in the workplace. The importance of developing professional connections to networking, career advancement, and business success is examined in this chapter. It draws attention to the tactical elements of establishing business relationships.

Chapter 8: Networking The Strategic Approach,

Building relationships intentionally and strategically involves networking. The deliberate endeavor to connect with others for either personal or professional reasons is referred to in this chapter as networking. It offers useful advice and methods for successful networking at occasions, conferences, and inside your company.

Chapter 9: Resolving Conflict

Any relationship will inevitably experience conflict. Conflict resolution is described in this chapter as the process of discussing and resolving conflicts in a constructive way. It looks at how to resolve disputes in a way that promotes growth and builds relationships.

Chapter 10: Building Personal Relationships,

The foundation of our emotional health is found in our interpersonal relationships. Personal relationships are those ties with friends, family, and loved ones, according to this chapter. It explores the mechanics of establishing and maintaining these connections while highlighting the significance of emotional intelligence.

Chapter 11: Emotional Intelligence in Relationship Building,

The capacity to identify, comprehend, and manage emotions—both our own and those of others—is known as emotional intelligence. This chapter examines the importance of emotional intelligence in developing relationships, emphasizing its role in forging stronger bonds and successfully resolving problems.

Chapter 12: Embracing Diversity and Inclusion
Building relationships across multiple backgrounds and viewpoints is essential in a world that is becoming more and more diverse. Diversity and inclusion are described in this chapter as the acceptance of different identities, backgrounds, and beliefs. It talks on the value of encouraging inclusive partnerships.

Chapter 13: Long-Distance and Online Relationships
Long-distance and online relationships are a common feature of modern living. In this chapter, these relationships are defined, and the special opportunities and problems they

bring are examined. It offers advice on how to keep deep friendships in the digital age.

Chapter 14: Taking Care of Long-Term Relationships

The longevity of a relationship over time is the actual test of its success. The definition of long-term partnerships and advice on fostering and preserving them are presented in this chapter. It highlights how crucial consistency, consideration, and flexibility are.

Chapter 15:Relationships in Leadership,

Relationships are fundamental to leadership. This chapter examines the crucial part relationships play in leadership, highlighting how strong relationships help effective leaders motivate teams, build trust, and foster a great work environment.

Chapter 16: Relationships' Legacy

Our connections leave a lasting impression. This chapter explains how relationships have a long-term effect and illustrates how the connections we make influence both our personal and professional legacies. It challenges readers to think about the legacy they want their interactions with others to leave behind.

Conclusion: The Continuous Process of Relationship Building
In conclusion, developing connections is a dynamic and diverse activity that improves both our own and other people's quality of life. It is art because it touches on the human heart, feelings, and connections that go beyond just business dealings. It qualifies as a science since its concepts and methods can be used to comprehend, cultivate, and master it.

A life that is enhanced by the depth of connections we create with others is one in which we are able to create and maintain meaningful relationships. Success in life is determined not just by our own accomplishments but also by the positive influence we have on people around us.

As we draw to a close this in-depth discussion of "Building Relationships," we are reminded that relationships are the foundation of our life. They provide us the strength to overcome obstacles in life, the comfort in difficult times, and the delight in happy occasions. Our lives and the lives of everyone we come in contact with are improved by the art and science of connection building. People will forget what you said and what you did, but they won't forget how you made them feel, as Maya Angelou once remarked.

Chapter 7

Balance and Well-being

The Art of Harmonizing Life: Finding Balance and Well-Being

Finding balance and wellbeing has become a desired but frequently elusive aim amid the hustle and bustle of the modern world, where demands and diversions are abundant. There are times when the need for balance in our lives can be overshadowed by the quest of achievement, self-improvement, and enjoyment. In this thorough investigation, we delve into the intricate web of balance and well-being, defining these ideas, highlighting their significance, and providing helpful advice for balancing all aspects of life in order to create a true state of well-being.

Chapter 1: The Search for Balance and Well-Being

Finding balance and wellbeing has become crucial in our fast-paced environment. In this chapter, the ideas of balance and wellbeing are introduced, with an emphasis on how important they are to living a happy and purposeful life. It emphasizes the connections between these ideas and how they support happiness and personal development.

Chapter 2: Balance Definition
In many facets of life, balance is frequently defined as stability or equilibrium. This chapter provides a thorough definition of balance with an emphasis on its function in managing competing demands, efficiently allocating time and resources, and lowering stress. It emphasizes that equilibrium is a dynamic, constantly changing process rather than a static condition.

Chapter 3: The Complexity of Well-Being
Physical, mental, and emotional health are all included in the concept of well-being. The

complex character of well-being is explored in this chapter, which defines it as a state of general contentment, vitality, and life satisfaction. It examines well-being's various facets, such as its physical, emotional, social, and psychological components.

The Play in Chapter 4 Between Harmony and Health
Well-being and balance go hand in hand. This chapter looks at the relationship between finding balance in different areas of life, including employment, relationships, health, and personal development. It highlights how an imbalance can cause stress, burnout, and a decline in general wellbeing.

Chapter 5: Striking a Balance Between Work and Life
Work-life harmony is crucial to overall equilibrium and wellbeing. Work-life balance is described in this chapter as the harmony of personal and professional obligations. It

covers the difficulties people have juggling the demands of work with those of personal and family life and offers solutions for finding balance.

Chapter 6: Caring for Your Body Physical Well-being
The basis of general well-being is physical health. In order to achieve a level of wellbeing, this chapter examines the significance of physical health, including diet, exercise, sleep, and stress management. It provides helpful advice for preserving physical wellness.

Chapter 7: Mental and Emotional Health
A person's total wellbeing depends on their emotional and mental health. The ability to effectively manage and regulate emotions, stress, and problems is the definition of emotional and mental well-being in this chapter. It talks about ways to improve one's mental health, resilience, and emotional intelligence.

Chapter 8: The Function of Social Connections

A crucial component of well being is social ties. This chapter investigates the value of friendships, connections, and social support in fostering wellbeing. It provides advice on creating and preserving enduring social bonds.

Chapter 9: Seeking Personal Development

A rewarding and transformational path is personal progress. Personal growth is described in this chapter as the ongoing process of learning about oneself and improving oneself. It talks on the value of making objectives, accepting difficulties, and developing a growth mentality.

Chapter 10: Finding Balance in the Digital Age,

In the digital age, successfully managing technology and digital distractions is essential for maintaining balance and wellbeing. This chapter provides advice on how to keep a positive relationship with technology, including time management, digital detox, and mindful tech use.

Chapter 11: Well-being and Mindfulness
The practice of mindfulness can significantly improve wellbeing. Being totally present and involved in the present moment is what is meant by mindfulness, according to this chapter. It looks at the role that mindfulness practices like meditation and mindful living can have in fostering emotional fortitude and general wellbeing.

Chapter 12: Strategies for Finding Balance
Balance involves deliberate actions and approaches. This chapter provides helpful advice on how to manage your time, set boundaries, and prioritize your own needs in order to achieve balance in different areas of your life. It highlights how crucial self-awareness and introspection are to this process.

Chapter 13: Developing Resilience
Being resilient means having the capacity to overcome challenges. Resilience is characterized in this chapter as a key component of preserving wellbeing in the face of adversity. It examines methods for fostering resilience, such as enhancing one's capacity for problem-solving and creating a solid network of allies.

Chapter 14: Building a Well-Being Plan,
A proactive step in achieving balance and well-being is developing a well-being strategy. This chapter helps readers develop a tailored well-being strategy that takes into account their particular requirements and objectives. It highlights the value of ongoing self-evaluation and correction.

Chapter 15: The Function of Gratitude and Positivity

Positive thinking and gratitude are crucial components of wellbeing. This section explains thankfulness

Chapter 8

Ethical Leadership

The CEO Chronicles: Creating a Legacy of Integrity and Impact via Ethical Leadership.
In the evolving corporate leadership landscape portrayed in the "CEO Chronicles," ethical leadership emerges as a defining quality of forward-thinking CEOs. In the framework of the CEO Chronicles, this exploration tries to define and explain the idea of ethical leadership by illuminating its significance, guiding principles, and practical applications. It demonstrates how moral leadership acts as a compass, assisting CEOs in navigating difficult situations, motivating staff, and leaving a long-lasting legacy of integrity and influence.

Chapter 1: The CEO Chronicles: Defining Ethical Leadership

The CEO Chronicles' central idea of ethical leadership serves as the narrative's compass. In order to set the scenario, this chapter provides a thorough description of ethical leadership. It emphasizes that moral integrity, honesty, fairness, and responsibility are the cornerstones of ethical leadership. It emphasizes how moral leaders put the health of their businesses, staff, and society at large first.

Chapter 2: The Moral Imperative of Ethical Leadership,

The moral obligation of ethical leadership makes it more than just a choice. The CEO Chronicles emphasize the moral obligations of CEOs. The moral aspects of ethical leadership are examined in this chapter, with a focus on the value of moral decision-making and the prevention of harm to stakeholders.

Chapter 3: Using ethical leadership as a beacon of trust,

The currency of leadership is trust, and the defender of trust is ethical leadership. This chapter explores the function of moral leaders in fostering trust. It discusses how fostering trust among coworkers, clients, investors, and the general public is accomplished through ethical leadership. It presents instances from the CEO Chronicles when trust gives an advantage over rivals in the real world.

chapter 4: Leading by Example: The CEO Chronicles' Ethical Icons,

CEOs who set an ethical example in the Chronicles are good examples of ethical leadership. This chapter offers a few moral role models from the CEO Chronicles and examines how their deeds and choices adhere to moral standards. It emphasizes their dedication to honesty and openness.

Chapter 5: The Process of Making Ethical Decisions
A methodical approach to decision-making is required for ethical leadership. The measures CEOs take to assess ethical quandaries, balance ethical factors, and make moral decisions are highlighted in this chapter's analysis of the ethical decision-making process. It exemplifies how moral leaders put long-term ethical results before immediate benefits.

Chapter 6: Promoting an Ethics Culture
Beyond the behaviors of one person, ethical leadership shapes the culture of the organization. This chapter examines how the CEOs in The CEO Chronicles foster an ethical environment within their businesses. In order to foster an ethical workplace, it is discussed how important it is to have clear ethical standards, policies, and training.

Chapter 7: The Balancing Act of the Ethical Leader

Complex ethical conundrums are frequently navigated in ethical leadership. This chapter sheds light on how CEOs strike a balance between conflicting interests and moral issues. It demonstrates their capacity to make challenging decisions that are consistent with their moral principles.

Chapter 8: Moral Leadership under Adversity

Crisis reveals a leader's genuine character. The CEO Chronicles shows how moral leaders excel under trying circumstances. This chapter examines how CEOs exercise moral leadership in times of crisis, placing special emphasis on accountability, openness, and crisis communication.

Chapter 9: Stakeholder-Centric Ethical Leadership,

All stakeholders are included in ethical leadership. This chapter explores how

CEOs in the CEO Chronicles give importance to the welfare of their people, their business, their shareholders, their communities, and the environment. The pursuit of common values and sustainability is emphasized as being essential to ethical leadership.

Chapter 10: Diversity & Inclusion and Ethical Leadership

It is ethically necessary to value diversity and inclusion. This chapter investigates how moral CEOs promote inclusiveness and diversity throughout their firms. It demonstrates the beneficial effects of diverse leadership teams on moral judgment and creativity.

Chapter 11: Corporate Social Responsibility and Ethical Leadership

Corporate social responsibility (CSR) and moral leadership are linked. CSR is described in this chapter as a dedication to moral business practices that advance society. It looks at how moral CEOs in the CEO Chronicles use CSR into their business plans to make a good social impact.

Chapter 12: The Long-Term Benefits of Ethical Leadership
Long-term success is an investment in ethical leadership. This chapter illustrates how moral leaders benefit from stakeholder trust, reputation, and long-term growth in the CEO Chronicles. It presents instances of CEOs who have rendered enduring models of moral leadership.

Chapter 13: Overcoming Ethical Challenges
There are obstacles to ethical leadership. In the CEO Chronicles, conflicts of interest and ethical breaches are among the common ethical problems that CEOs deal with. It provides instructions on how moral leaders should approach and solve these problems.

Chapter 14: The Legacy of the Ethical Leader

Creating a legacy is an important part of ethical leadership; it goes beyond the here and now. In the CEO Chronicles, this chapter examines the enduring legacy of moral leaders. It underlines how ethical leadership has a lasting impact on companies and society even after a person has left office.

The Long-Lasting Effect of Ethical Leadership

In the CEO Chronicles, ethical leadership shines as a beacon of integrity and significance. It captures the essence of forward-thinking CEOs who put moral values first, build trust, and make moral choices. A path to long-term success and a legacy of ethical influence, ethical leadership is not an option but an ethical duty. John C. Maxwell once said that "a leader is one who knows the way, goes the way, and shows the way." This idea is embodied by ethical executives in the CEO Chronicles, who run their companies with unshakeable morality and leave a lasting mark on society.

Chapter 9

Measuring Success

Determining, Evaluating, and Achieving Excellence: Measuring Success

The desire to gauge success is a continuous companion in the quest for both personal and professional development. It is a journey with many facets, and different people, cultures, and settings define it differently. Success is a reflection of our beliefs, goals, and aspirations rather than merely an accomplishment. In this in-depth investigation, we will define, evaluate, and investigate the nuances of success measurement. We'll look into the components of success, how it changes over time, the importance of personal definitions, and how to set goals for excelling in different areas of life.

Chapter 1: The Ever-Evolving Notion of Success,
Success is an ever-changing, dynamic idea. The concept of success as a fluid, ever-changing destination influenced by one's own development, societal changes, and shifting desires is introduced in this chapter. It emphasizes how crucial adaptation is while gauging and pursuing success.

Chapter 2: Beyond Conventional Wisdom: Defining Success
Success is a highly individualized concept. This chapter examines the definition of success while highlighting the value of personal viewpoints. It talks about how cultural and societal conventions can affect how we see success and how crucial it is to match our own definitions of success with our own values.

Chapter 3: The Multidimensional Nature of Success,

Success is multifaceted; it includes many different aspects of life. This chapter explores the multifaceted nature of success and how it might appear in areas including career, relationships, personal growth, health, and social contribution. It emphasizes how crucial it is to strike a balance between these aspects.

Chapter 4: Metrics and Measures for Evaluating Success

We need measurements and measures to assess success. This chapter explores the numerous metrics that can be used to measure success, from quantitative ones like monetary gains and professional milestones to qualitative ones like impact on others and personal fulfillment. It underlines the necessity of an all-encompassing evaluation strategy.

Chapter 5: The Importance of Goal Setting for Success Measuring

Setting goals is essential for determining success and accomplishing it. The significance of establishing specific, meaningful goals that are consistent with one's idea of success is covered in this chapter. It examines goal-setting strategies, including SMART objectives, and their function in offering guidance and inspiration.

Chapter 6: The Influence of Self-Evaluation

A reflective approach that helps measure success is self-assessment. The function of self-assessment in monitoring advancement toward personal and professional objectives is examined in this chapter. It addresses techniques for self-evaluation include journaling, introspection, and requesting feedback.

Chapter 7: Personal Growth and Success

Success and personal development go hand in hand. Personal development is described in this chapter as a continuous process of growth and progress. It looks at how making personal development investments can help people become more resilient, self-aware, and able to adjust to change—essential qualities for success.

Chapter 8: Success in Career and Professional Life,
A key component of overall success is career success. This chapter looks at how work success can be defined and assessed, taking into account things like job happiness, career advancement, recognition, and compatibility with personal values. Additionally, the idea of work-life balance is covered.

Chapter 9: Success in Relationships and Your Personal Life
Relationships are often the key to personal success. This chapter examines how communication, closeness, trust, and mutual support can be used to gauge a

relationship's success. It explores the value of fostering deep bonds with loved ones, friends, and lovers.

Chapter 10: Success and well-being
Success has a vital component called well-being. This chapter examines the relationship between well-being and overall success by defining it as a state of physical, mental, and emotional health. In order to achieve wellbeing, it addresses the value of self-care, stress reduction, and mindfulness.

Chapter 11: Achievement and Social Impact
A strong indicator of success is one's ability to contribute to society. This chapter explores how acts of service, charity, and good societal influence might be used to define and assess success. It emphasizes the satisfaction gained from improving the lives of others.

Chapter 12: Success and Financial Prosperity,

Success and financial prosperity are frequently equated. The connection between monetary success and general well-being is examined in this chapter. In order to achieve financial goals as a measure of success, it is important to engage in financial planning, budgeting, and investment.

Chapter 13: Achievement and Fortitude

A key component in determining and achieving success is resilience. Resilience is described in this chapter as the capacity to overcome hardship and setbacks. It looks at how obstacles and failures can help build resilience, which ultimately aids in long-term success.

Chapter 14: Achieving Success Despite Obstacles

There will always be challenges in the path to success. This chapter lists frequent roadblocks to achievement, such as self-doubt, fear of failure, and external impediments. It provides advice on how to get over them while stressing the value of tenacity and adaptability.

Chapter 15: A Lifelong Journey to Success
Success is a lifelong journey rather than a destination. This chapter examines the notion that determining success is a dynamic process that changes with time and with experience. It urges readers to constantly reevaluate their ideas of success and to accept the fluidity of achievement.

In conclusion, success measurement is an art.
Finally, evaluating success is a highly individual and dynamic process. It's a path that necessitates introspection, flexibility, and self-awareness. Success includes many different aspects of life, such as personal development, interpersonal connections,

wellbeing, and societal contribution, and is not just measured by conventional metrics.

Setting meaningful goals, tracking progress, and overcoming challenges with resiliency and determination are all key components of the art of measuring success. Success is a diverse, always changing destination that reflects our individual routes, desires, and contributions to the world, not a set point on the horizon.

As we draw to a close this in-depth examination of "Measuring Success," we are reminded that success is not a single notion but a kaleidoscope of dimensions, each of which contributes to a full and purposeful existence. This journey, which is enriched by self-discovery, development, and the quest of excellence, eventually determines our legacy as a group and as individuals.

Chapter 10

Lessons Learned

Wisdom from Visionary Leaders: Lessons from the CEO Chronicles

Through the stories of forward-thinking CEOs, The "CEO Chronicles" unfolds a compelling narrative of leadership, innovation, and resiliency. This book offers insights that go beyond the boundaries of the corporate world by weaving priceless lessons into the tapestry of their adventures. This investigation looks deeply into the CEO Chronicles' teachings, illuminating the knowledge, values, and tactics that have molded these exceptional leaders.

Chapter 1: The Power of Vision,

Vision serves as the compass for visionary leaders. The CEO Chronicles highlight the importance of having a distinct and appealing vision. This chapter examines the role that a clear vision plays in guiding teams, motivating action, and advancing businesses toward excellence.

Chapter 2: Resilience in the Face of Adversity,
Leadership inevitably involves facing challenges. The CEO Chronicles demonstrate how developing resilience is a crucial life skill acquired through hardships. This chapter highlights the value of resilience in overcoming obstacles, picking yourself up after mistakes, and moving forward resolutely.

Chapter 3:;Embracing Change and Innovation
Progress is fueled by innovation. CEOs in the Chronicles are aware of how important it is to embrace change and promote innovation. This chapter explains how forward-thinking leaders foster an innovative culture, adjust to shifting conditions, and remain innovative.

Chapter 4: The Art of Decision-Making
Leadership is based on the ability to make decisions. The CEO Chronicles offer insightful perspectives on the art of decision-making. This chapter explores the tactics and guidelines CEOs use to arrive at wise, timely judgments that advance their companies.

Chapter 5: Developing a High-Performing Team
Every effective CEO has a strong team working for them. The Chronicles place a strong emphasis on the value of building and guiding teams well. The characteristics of good leadership, such as communication, trust, teamwork, and empowerment, are covered in this chapter.

Chapter 6: Ethics and Integrity in Leadership,
Visionary leaders uphold the non-negotiable standards of ethics and integrity. The CEO Chronicles emphasize the key takeaways

regarding the value of moral leadership. This chapter explains how trust and respect are built on the pillars of integrity, honesty, and ethical decision-making.

Chapter 7: Building Stable Relationships, Leadership is centered on relationships. The Chronicles show how CEOs give stakeholders' connections first priority. The art of networking, making connections, and cultivating deep ties are all topics covered in this chapter.

Chapter 8: The Balancing Act of Work and Life,
A common problem is juggling work and personal obligations. The Chronicles offer perspectives on how CEOs manage this precarious balance. In this chapter, methods for attaining balance between personal and professional lives are discussed, with a focus on self-care, boundaries, and wellbeing.

Chapter 9: Lessons in Communication,
An essential component of leadership is effective communication. The CEO Chronicles emphasize the knowledge gained regarding the effectiveness of communication. The art of effective communication is explored in this chapter along with active listening, transparency, and adaptation.

Chapter 10: Personal Development Techniques
For visionary leaders, personal development is a lifelong endeavor. The Chronicles offer insightful guidance on ongoing self-improvement. Setting objectives, getting feedback, and embracing lifelong learning are all discussed in this chapter.

Chapter 11: Navigating Global Challenges,
CEOs have particular difficulties in today's globalized society. The Chronicles provide guidance for negotiating the world's complexity. This chapter examines

approaches to addressing global concerns, cross-cultural leadership, and worldwide expansion.

Chapter 12: Giving Back: Corporate Social Responsibility,
The Chronicles teach readers the importance of giving back to the community. The significance of corporate social responsibility (CSR) and the beneficial effects CEOs can have on their communities and the world are covered in this chapter.

Chapter 13: The Leadership Legacy
The abiding hallmark of visionary leaders is legacy. The Chronicles offer guidance on creating a legacy. This chapter examines how CEOs create an enduring legacy through acting, making choices, and making contributions to society and their enterprises.

Chapter 14: Challenges and the Potential for Transformation

Challenges serve as growth's catalyst. The Chronicles show how CEOs convert obstacles into chances. This chapter talks about how adversity may change you and how it makes you more resilient.

Chapter 15: Humanity's Lessons

The Chronicles are frequently used to teach humility. This chapter examines how humility can be a source of strength, allowing CEOs to embrace other viewpoints, learn from others, and admit mistakes.

Chapter 16: The Art of Giving and Receiving Feedback,

An essential component of growth is feedback. The Chronicles offer perceptions on the craft of providing and receiving criticism. In this chapter, we'll talk about how efficient feedback mechanisms help people and organizations grow.

Chapter 17: Complexity Management Techniques

Leadership always involves a certain amount of complexity. The Chronicles provide methods for successfully handling complexity. This chapter examines the ways in which CEOs reduce complexity, rely on data when making choices, and maintain clarity under pressure.

Chapter 18: Lessons in Adaptability,

Visionary leaders have perfected the ability to adapt. The Chronicles place a strong emphasis on the value of flexibility in a world that is changing quickly. This chapter looks at how CEOs may remain flexible, change course when necessary, and lead with agility.

Chapter 19: Lessons Learned through Failures and Mistakes

Failure and mistakes are excellent lessons. The Chronicles show how CEOs improve after making mistakes. This chapter examines failure-related wisdom, failure-related resiliency, and the humility to admit mistakes.

Chapter 20: Constantly pursuing excellence
The ultimate goal of visionary leaders is excellence. The Chronicles encourage a never-ending quest for perfection. The lessons learnt about having high standards, encouraging an excellence-oriented culture, and never settling for mediocrity are explored in this chapter.

The Long-Term Effects of the Lessons Learned
The CEO Chronicles are a gold mine of knowledge, illustrating the lessons discovered by forward-thinking CEOs, to sum up. These teachings cover the art of leadership, perseverance through hardship, flexibility through change, and unshakable dedication to greatness. These teachings have a lasting effect on many aspects of life and go beyond the business world.

As we come to an end with our examination of "Lessons Learned from the CEO Chronicles," we are reminded that wise leadership is the legacy of visionary leaders. Their experiences motivate us to take on obstacles, act honorably as leaders, and constantly pursue excellence. These lessons are not only found in books; they are also woven into the fabric of leadership, creating a lasting impression on the world.

Conclusion:

Putting a Bold Course Into the Future in Conclusion

We have learned the keys to visionary leadership, seen the strength of resilience, and embraced the values of innovation and moral stewardship in the grand conclusion of the CEO Chronicles. As we come to an exciting conclusion, remember that it's not the end but rather the beginning of new adventures.

The Chronicles have outlined the road to success as a dynamic, ever-evolving journey rather than a far-off goal. They have demonstrated that leadership is a call to inspire, direct, and empower rather than a label. They have left us with a lasting impression of the value of unshakable morality, building connections, and leaving a legacy of trust.

Now that we have the knowledge of the Chronicles, we set out on our own journeys, creating tales of inspiration, tenacity, and impact. We learn from the lessons that success is a team effort rather than an individual one. We welcome the challenge to innovate with fervor, adapt with elegance, and lead with integrity.

Let's keep in mind that every ending ushers in a brand-new beginning as we turn the last page of the CEO Chronicles. The adventures that await us are limitless, and our journeys have yet to be written. We set sail towards the future with the Chronicles as our compass, prepared to reshape the world with purpose, resiliency, and steadfast principles.

Even if the CEO Chronicles have come to a close, our personal Chronicles have only just begun. Let's move forward with a vision in our hearts, fortitude in our souls, and the determination to leave a legacy that will motivate future generations.

Acknowledgments

The journey of writing the "CEO Chronicles" was one of inspiration, education, and cooperation. We want to express our sincere gratitude to everyone who helped make this book possible as we draw to a close.

First and foremost, we want to thank the inspirational CEOs whose experiences and advice helped to bring life to this book's pages. The "CEO Chronicles" have been built on your knowledge, experiences, and commitment to leadership. Your willingness to share your experiences is a gift to everyone who wants to lead with integrity and purpose.

We would also want to express our appreciation to the hardworking group who worked behind the scenes, including the editors, researchers, and designers whose relentless efforts made this book possible. Your dedication to quality and careful attention to detail have made sure that readers connect with the Chronicles.

We would want to express our gratitude to our families and close friends for their constant support, tolerance, and understanding during this writing process. Your support has served as our compass and your faith in our mission has strengthened our resolve.

We would like to express our sincere gratitude to our readers for traveling with us on this adventure. We will keep sharing tales that inspire and empower others because of your interest, engagement, and passion for leadership.

Finally, we want to thank all of the people who have helped us along the way as authors. Our viewpoints and passion of storytelling have been greatly shaped by your mentoring, support, and direction.

With thankful hearts, we draw to a close the "CEO Chronicles," confident that the lessons discovered and the knowledge imparted will endure and inspire leadership endeavors for years to come.